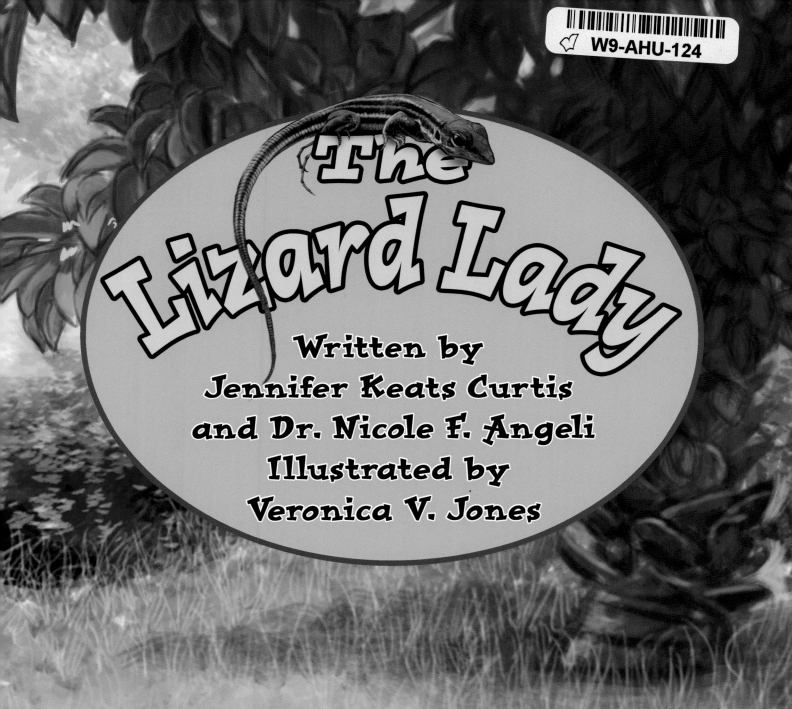

The Lizard Lady

Written by
Jennifer Keats Curtis
and Dr. Nicole F. Angeli
Illustrated by
Veronica V. Jones

Dr. Nicole F. Angeli is permitted to touch the critically endangered St. Croix ground lizard because she applied and was approved to study the animals under the Endangered Species Act (TE25057B-0). For anybody else to touch or harass a St. Croix ground lizard, or any endangered species, is called "take of the species" and is illegal!

Many others work to save St. Croix ground lizards as well, including the U.S. Fish and Wildlife Service's Caribbean Ecological Services and Refuges, Texas A&M University, the Virgin Islands Department of Planning and Natural Resources, and the U.S. National Park Service. Conservation biology is largely about teamwork!

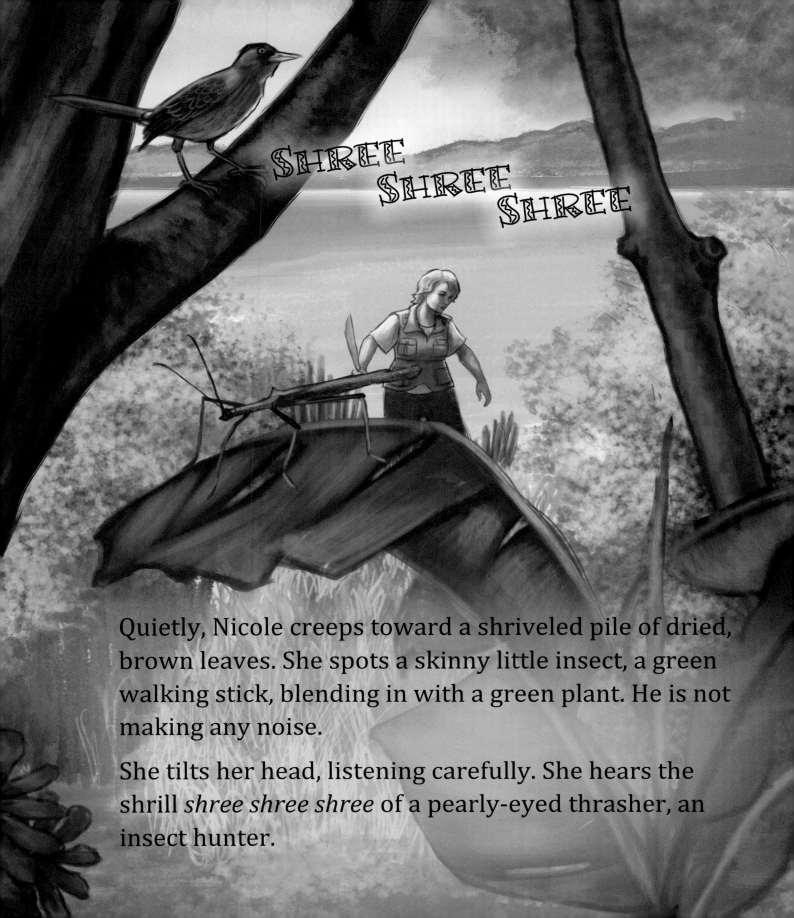

SHREE SHREE SHREE

Quietly, Nicole creeps toward a shriveled pile of dried, brown leaves. She spots a skinny little insect, a green walking stick, blending in with a green plant. He is not making any noise.

She tilts her head, listening carefully. She hears the shrill *shree shree shree* of a pearly-eyed thrasher, an insect hunter.

Nicole sweeps thorns from her pants. She wipes the sweat from her face. It is time to get out of the blinding sun. With a sigh, she sits in the shade of a cactus and sips her water.

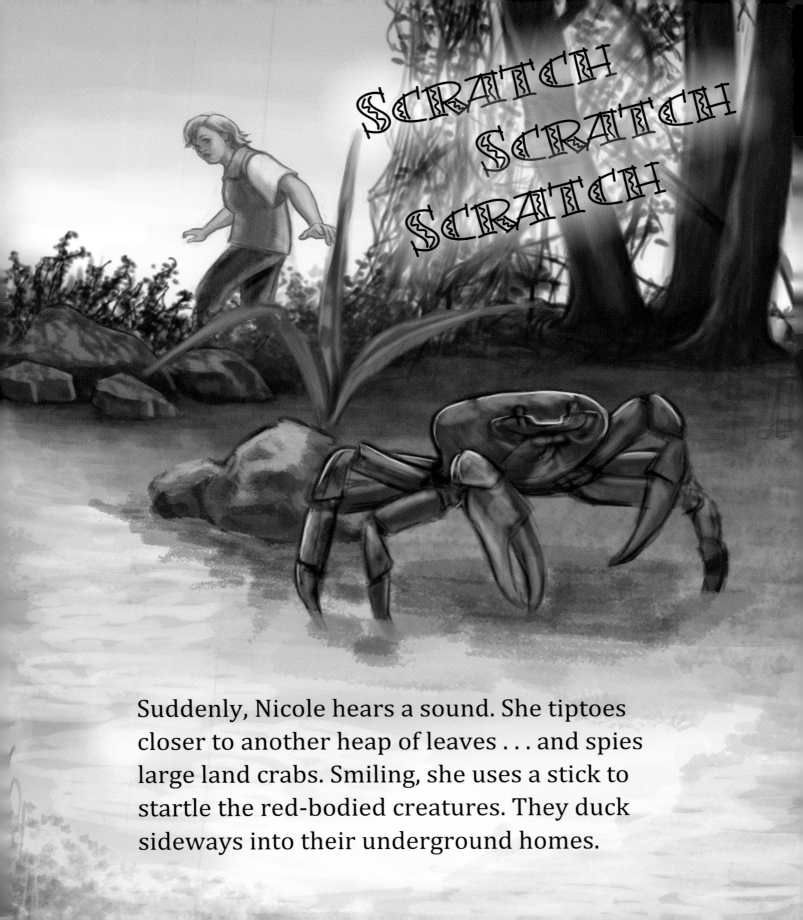

SCRATCH
SCRATCH
SCRATCH

Suddenly, Nicole hears a sound. She tiptoes closer to another heap of leaves . . . and spies large land crabs. Smiling, she uses a stick to startle the red-bodied creatures. They duck sideways into their underground homes.

Nicole is not looking for insects or crabs. She is searching for a critically endangered animal, the St. Croix ground lizard.

Nicole is a scientist who
studies these lizards. The
people on the islands call her
the Lizard Lady.

The Lizard Lady searches for St. Croix ground lizards on four small islands around St. Croix in the U.S. Virgin Islands.

Why aren't they on St. Croix?

In the 1880s, farmers on St. Croix brought mongooses to the island. The farmers thought the mongooses would eat the rats that were eating their sugarcane crops.

The mongooses didn't eat all the rats.
The rats climbed trees to get away.
Mongooses can't climb well, so instead
they ate sea turtle eggs. And birds.
And almost every St. Croix ground
lizard on St. Croix.

The ground lizards will never be able to live on St. Croix again, unless all of the mongooses are removed. Fortunately, the lizards have survived on two little islands—Protestant Cay and Green Cay.

To save these little reptiles from extinction, scientists planned to bring St. Croix ground lizards from the two cays to two new homes on nearby Ruth Island and Buck Island. Did their idea work?

Today, the Lizard Lady has
come to Buck Island to find out.

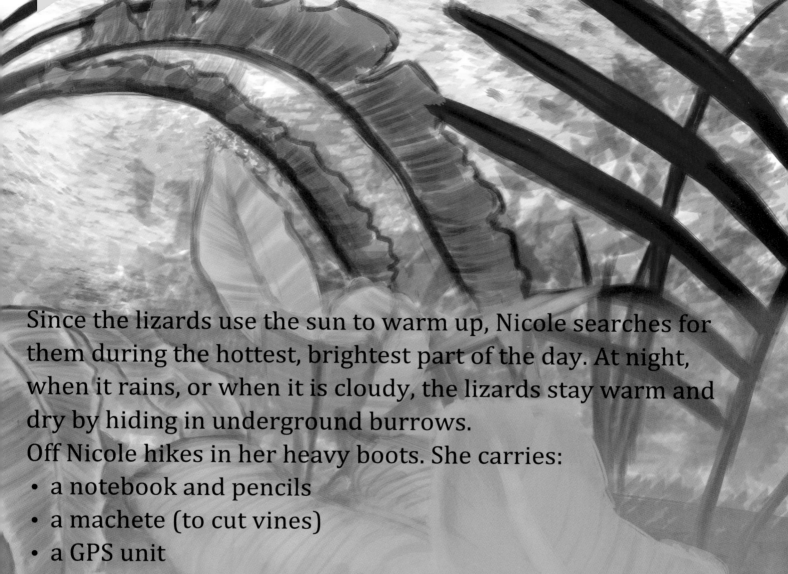

Since the lizards use the sun to warm up, Nicole searches for them during the hottest, brightest part of the day. At night, when it rains, or when it is cloudy, the lizards stay warm and dry by hiding in underground burrows.

Off Nicole hikes in her heavy boots. She carries:

- a notebook and pencils
- a machete (to cut vines)
- a GPS unit
- flagging tape (in case her GPS unit doesn't work)
- a cell phone
- a whistle (in case her phone doesn't work)
- a small empty cooler (to safely store the lizards)
- a gallon of water

The Lizard Lady hikes over ridge tops, into the dense Caribbean forest, and across sandy beaches. She uses the machete to whack her way through thick plants, heavy brush, and sometimes giant spider webs.

The lizards are hard to see, but Nicole is an expert tracker. Sometimes, she hears the lizards before she can even see them.

Shhh! Do you hear that?

A lizard is hungrily prowling, looking for small prey—cockroaches, crickets, moths, termites, ants, and small hermit crabs—in the leaves.

There! Nicole sees two tiny eyes of an alert lizard watching her. Using a long pole with a knotted loop on the end, Nicole slowly slips the rope over its head. As it tightens, the reptile rolls to get away. Quickly, before it escapes, Nicole snatches its belly and legs.

This one is feisty! St. Croix ground lizards have sharp, serrated teeth; but they are small, so Nicole doesn't mind a curious nibble of her fingers.

Nicole carefully drops the lizard into her cooler before recording the GPS coordinates and tying flagging tape on a branch. She packs up her gear and heads to a shack near the beach. There, she keeps a ruler, a scale, and her notebook. She measures and weighs the lizard.

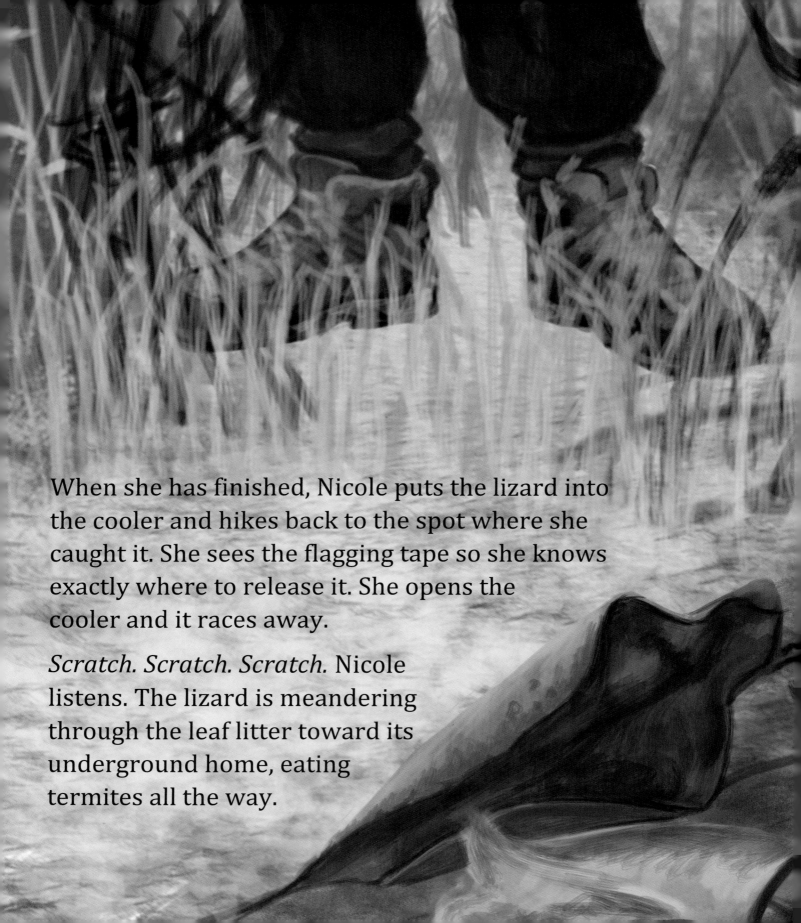

When she has finished, Nicole puts the lizard into the cooler and hikes back to the spot where she caught it. She sees the flagging tape so she knows exactly where to release it. She opens the cooler and it races away.

Scratch. Scratch. Scratch. Nicole listens. The lizard is meandering through the leaf litter toward its underground home, eating termites all the way.

The idea to move the lizards is working! But the work is not done. The Lizard Lady is among a group of scientists who monitor the lizards each year.

These lizards live on small islands, without mongooses. One day, if the mongooses are removed from St. Croix, the lizards could return to their native island. But not today. Today, it is time for the Lizard Lady to go home.

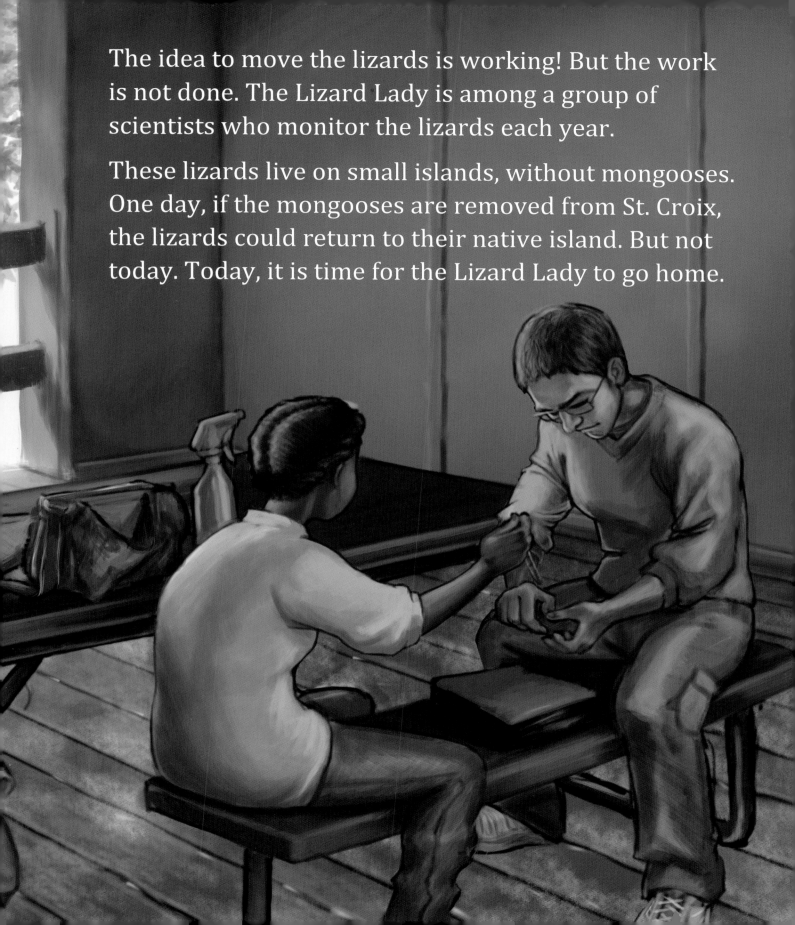

Nicole turns on the boat's engine and unties it from the dock. As she leaves the island behind, a flock of brown pelicans soars overhead. She spots a sea turtle surfacing to take a breath. Over the bow, flying fish glint like silver flashes.

It is just another day in the life of the Lizard Lady.

For Creative Minds

St. Croix and Surrounding Islands

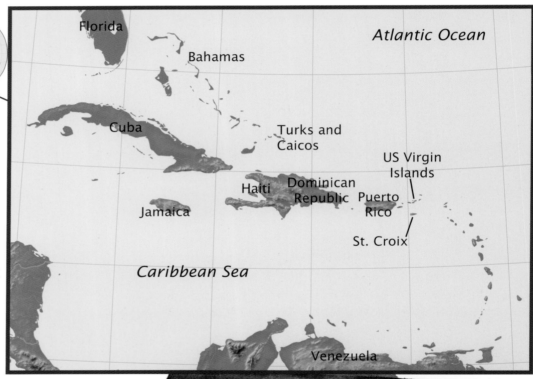

The Caribbean is a sea between North and South America. St. Croix is one of more than 7,000 islands in the Caribbean Sea.

There are 28 island countries in the Caribbean. But St. Croix is not an independent country. It is part of the US Virgin Islands, a territory of the United States. Puerto Rico is also a US territory.

Map Questions

1. The Dominican Republic is on the same island as what other country?
2. What ocean is to the east of the Caribbean Sea?
3. What country is just south of Florida?
4. What island or cay is south of St. Croix?
5. Where is Buck Island in relation to St. Croix?

St. Croix Ground Lizards

The St. Croix ground lizard is a St. Croix native. In fact, these lizards are **endemic** to St. Croix. That means that they are not naturally found anywhere in the world except for St. Croix.

St. Croix ground lizards currently live on four islands: Protestant Cay, Green Cay, Ruth Island and Buck Island. Long ago, Protestant Cay and Green Cay were part of the island of St. Croix. These two cays are part of the lizards' natural habitat. The lizards live on Ruth Island and Buck Island only because they have been taken there by people. This is called a **conservation translocation**.

These lizards are critically endangered. If we do not help them, they could become extinct.

Adaptations

Adaptations are changes that allow some animals to survive better than other animals in their environment. Physical adaptations affect the animals' bodies. Animal parents pass these adaptations on to their young. The young animals grow up and pass their adaptations on to kids of their own. Behavioral adaptations affect the way the animals act.

Like many other animals, St. Croix ground lizards use physical and behavioral adaptations to search for food and avoid predators. Sort the following traits into physical or behavioral.

1. St. Croix ground lizards have light brown, dark brown, and white stripes down their back. This pattern helps the lizards hide in the leaves.

St. Croix ground lizards race into underground burrows to hide from predators. **2.**

3. St. Croix ground lizards have a forked tongue to smell things around them.

St. Croix ground lizards sniff the ground to find food or other lizards. **4.**

Physical: 1 and 3. Behavioral: 2 and 4.

Dr. Nicole F. Angeli, Herpetologist

As a girl, I wanted to be an explorer! I loved discovering everything in the great outdoors. I never wanted to be inside. I'd forage for insects, animals, and berries and look for sticks to whittle. I always knew that I'd become a scientist but what kind? In school, I learned that I didn't want to be in a lab. I wanted to be outside. Being a herpetologist—a scientist who studies reptiles and amphibians—allows me to spend most of my time outdoors. My passion is conserving animals. I love learning why some species survive while others go extinct and figuring out ways to save threatened animals, like the St. Croix ground lizard.

Even on weekends, I am a herpetologist. Anyone can be a herpetologist. All you need is an interest in reptiles and amphibians and a notebook! Open your notebook, and create columns for the date, weather, place, species, photo ID, and notes on the right-hand page. Keep the left hand page for your notes. On each page, write the date and location across the top. Then write about the amphibians and reptiles you see.

—Dr. Nicole F. Angeli

If you like working in groups, check out a club near you so that you can detect, identify, and manage yourself safely around scaly and slimy friends. The Society for the Study of Amphibians and Reptiles (www.ssarherps.org) keeps an updated list of local herpetological societies. Contact them to learn more.

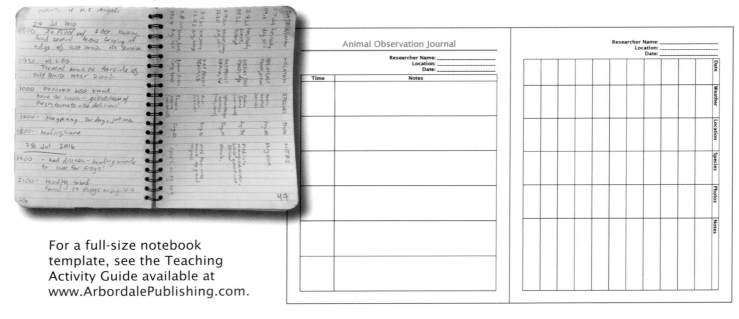

For a full-size notebook template, see the Teaching Activity Guide available at www.ArbordalePublishing.com.

Invasive Species

In the late 1800s, farmers in St. Croix brought Indian mongooses to get rid of rats on the island. These small, furry mammals might be cute, but they are among the top ten most harmful **invasive species**. Invasive species are not native animals. They cause problems for native animals or the environment.

Mongooses are predators, and they are destructive. They have eaten so many St. Croix ground lizards that we are in danger of losing this species forever. Mongooses also chomp down on the eggs of lots of other animals, like sea turtles and sea birds.

Today, mongooses live on about 99% of the land in the Caribbean. They are mostly found on the larger islands. We can conserve native animals by helping them move to small islands without any mongooses.

Invasive Species often

- hunt native species
- reproduce quickly
- spread out to cover a wide territory
- can live in many different types of habitats
- are often introduced to an area by humans

Dr. Angeli and her team have come up with ways to save the St. Croix ground lizard from extinction. They need to be creative to find conservation methods that don't cost a lot of money. They find or create areas where no mongooses live or where mongooses are separated from the lizards by a fence. In the future, Dr. Angeli hopes to return the St. Croix ground lizards to St. Croix.

To extraordinary teachers, Rebecca Dobson, Krystal Schlissler and Erin Johnson, who so willingly share their knowledge in and out of the classroom.—JKC

To my nephews, Joseph and Michael. That they may have the sturdy, educational, and marvelous upbringing that their grandparents gave to my sister and me.—NFA

For my wonderful supportive family.—VVJ

Thanks to Dr. Robert Powell, Professor of Biology at Avila University, for verifying the accuracy of the information in this book.

Library of Congress Cataloging-in-Publication Data

Names: Curtis, Jennifer Keats, author. | Angeli, Nicole F., author. | Jones, Veronica, illustrator.
Title: The lizard lady / by Jennifer Keats Curtis and Dr. Nicole F. Angeli ; illustrated by Veronica V. Jones.
Description: Mount Pleasant, [South Carolina] : Arbordale, [2018] | Audience: Ages 4-8. | Audience: K to grade 3. | Includes bibliographical references.
Identifiers: LCCN 2017040946 (print) | LCCN 2017049453 (ebook) | ISBN 9781607183150 (English Downloadable eBook) | ISBN 9781607183174 (English Interactive Dual-Language eBook) | ISBN 9781607183167 (Spanish Downloadable eBook) | ISBN 9781607183181 (Spanish Interactive Dual-Language eBook) | ISBN 9781607180661 (english hardcover) | ISBN 9781607180913 (english pbk.) | ISBN 9781607183112 (spanish pbk.)
Subjects: LCSH: Angeli, Nicole F.--Juvenile literature. | Herpetologists--Juvenile literature. | Women scientists--United States Virgin Islands--Juvenile literature. | Ameiva--Conservation--Juvenile literature. | Rare reptiles--Conservation--United States Virgin Islands--Saint Croix--Juvenile literature. | Saint Croix (United States Virgin Islands)--Juvenile literature.
Classification: LCC QL31.A5845 (ebook) | LCC QL31.A5845 C87 2018 (print) | DDC 333.95/72097297/22--dc23
LC record available at https://lccn.loc.gov/2017040946

Translated into Spanish: *La dama de las Siguanas*

Lexile® Level: 830L

key phrases: Environmental education, helping animals, threatened and endangered species, conservation, scientist, women in STEM,

Bibliography:
Angeli, N. F. Ameiva polops (Saint Croix Ameiva). 2013. Conservation. Caribbean Herpetology 45 (1).
Angeli, N. F., K. Auer, N. Schwartz, Z. Westfall, C. Pollock, I. Lundgren, and Z. Hillis-Starr. 2013. Ameiva polops (St. Croix Ground Lizard) Behavior. Herpetological Review 44 (3): 504.
Fitzgerald, L., Treglia, M., Angeli, N., Hibbitts, T., Leavitt, D., Subalusky, A., Lundgren, L., and Hillis-Starr, Z. 2015. Determinants of successful establishment and post-translocation dispersal of a new population of the critically endangered St. Croix ground lizard (Ameiva polops). Restoration Ecology. 23(5): 776-786.

Manufactured in China, December 2017
This product conforms to CPSIA 2008
First Printing

Arbordale Publishing
Mt. Pleasant, SC 29464
www.ArbordalePublishing.com